Californian Architecture
in
Santa Barbara

SANTA BARBARA MISSION

RESTORED BY ROSS MONTGOMERY,
ARCHITECT.

Californian Architecture
in
Santa Barbara

H. PHILIP STAATS

ROWMAN & LITTLEFIELD PUBLISHERS, INC.
Lanham • Boulder • New York • Toronto • Plymouth, UK

Published by Rowman & Littlefield Publishers, Inc.
A wholly owned subsidary of The Rowman & Littlefield Publishing Group, Inc.
4501 Forbes Boulevard, Suite 200, Lanham, Maryland 20706
www.rowman.com

10 Thornbury Road, Plymouth PL6 7PP, United Kingdom

Distributed by National Book Network

British Library Cataloguing in Publication Information Available

The previous edition of this book was cataloged by the Library of Congress as follows:

Californian architecture in Santa Barbara / collected and edited by H. Philip Staats ; with a
    new preface by Charles H. Cheney ; introduction to new edition by David Gebhard.
    —New ed.
        p. cm.
    1. Architecture—California—Santa Barbara. 2. Architecture, Spanish colonial—
California—Santa Barbara. 3. Eclecticism in architecture—California—Santa Barbara.
    4. Santa Barbara (Calif.)—Buildings, structures, etc. I. Staats, H. Philip.
    NA735.S42C35   1989
    720'.9794'91—dc19   89–6497

ISBN 978-1-4422-2427-8 (pbk. : alk. paper)
ISBN 978-1-4422-2428-5 (electronic)

∞™ The paper used in this publication meets the minimum requirements of American
National Standard for Information Sciences—Permanence of Paper for Printed Library
Materials, ANSI/NISO Z39.48-1992.

Printed in the United States of America

Californian Architecture in Santa Barbara

WHAT is more natural than to find the full flower of Californian Architecture in Santa Barbara. For up the channel, fifty years after Columbus had discovered America, Cabrillo sailed on his first voyage of discovery, to claim the western country for the King of Spain. But for two hundred and fifty years after this it lay forgotten, occupied only by the native Indians, until towards the end of the eighteenth century rumors came of the Russians settling in Alaska and along the northern shore, when the Spanish government thought it time to protect its California claims. Little bands of troops were landed at different points, a presidio was built at Santa Barbara, and under its protection the Franciscans in 1786 founded a mission, one of the chain, "one day's march apart," from Mexico to Sonoma north of San Francisco Bay. With them they brought a wealth of culture and the developed art of Latin civilization, where architecture had for centuries been adapting itself to a similar climate along the Mediterranean. The first mission church in Santa Barbara was small and crude, to be followed in a few years by a second, which in turn was abandoned for the present structure of stone finished in 1820, one of the most beautiful and best preserved of all the Missions, and which has had its influence in the spread of the so called "Mission Architecture" in California.

The cool broad patios, thick adobe walls, soft warm colored tile roofs, as well as the large flat tile of the floors, were well suited to comfortable living in this part of the world, and they have had a great effect upon the present day architecture of a more complex civilization.

California's second romantic period came with the rush of gold seekers in 1849, a year after the new territory became part of the United States as a result of the war with Mexico. New England sea captains had brought around the Horn before this time wooden houses and whole buildings designed in the Georgian or American-Colonial style and set them up at Monterey, San Francisco and other coastal points.

At Monterey particularly there soon came to be an architecture depicting a pleasant fusion of the cultures of the two civilizations— the heavier Spanish type with little refinement of detail and ornament (because their workmen were practically all Indians of little or no training and no tools) as contrasting with the slender delicate mouldings and clear cut lines of well trained American carpenters and wood workers. However, it was not until the railroad came through Santa Barbara in the 80's, to link up Los Angeles and San Francisco, that the unusual beauty of this location and climate began to appeal to people of wealth and leisure. Then great leaders of finance and fashion settled here, until Santa Barbara with its neighboring communities now has one of the most notable groups in America of large country places and of fine small houses. Yet with it all there is a most pleasing simplicity, a lack of ostentation and display in this quiet California community not found in any other place in America. It has combined the precious harmony and restfulness and much of the dignity and color of its inherited Latin culture, with some of the best of that American architecture which is so largely dominated in other parts of the country by English precedent.

Marvelous gardens grow in this region because of the very slight difference in temperature between summer and winter. Fortunately a great plant specialist, an Italian, Dr. Franceschi Fenzi, nearly forty years ago began to introduce rare and beautiful flowering trees and shrubs from the far corners of the earth, which have now grown to great size. One may see in Santa Barbara perhaps the largest range of ornamental trees and floral culture to be found outside the one or two great botanic gardens of the United States. This wealth of plant material has inspired the landscape architects and gardeners in Santa Barbara, and also the home owners, so that even around small houses there is foliage, color, and a setting that enhances the architecture to a greater degree than we are accustomed to elsewhere. A distinguished grower of hybrids in Santa Barbara once told me that the first time he stepped off the train in mid winter and saw the great bed of orange lantana in full bloom in the station garden he knew that this was the place for him to spend the rest of his life.

All styles of architecture are of course to be found in a community where so many people have been transplanted, so few grown up with it from its birth. With them have also come some transplanted tastes, perhaps appropriate to snow countries and other climates, good and bad tastes, with sometimes preconceived ideas that are difficult to adjust. But there is in Santa Barbara less of the usual jumble of styles and tastes in architecture than in other similar American communities. The Latin solution well adapted to the climate, made a strong appeal and naturally this style predominates.

Californian Architecture Defined

Thus there has flowered in Santa Barbara some of the best of the architecture come to be called "Californian." For this term the following description is beginning commonly to be accepted:—

"Californian Architecture is defined as that distinctive style which for several decades has been successfully growing up in this State, deriving its chief inspiration directly or indirectly from Latin types which developed under similar climatic conditions along the Mediterranean, or at points in Mexico and California.

"Color is generally very light in tone.

"Materials used are plaster, adobe or stucco exterior wall surfaces of durable construction, or of concrete, stone or artificial stone.

"Roofs are low pitched, seldom steeper than thirty degrees, with thirty-five degrees maximum, usually of tile laid random, but sometimes in the galleried Monterey type, using shakes or shingles, often with thick butts."

The most remarkable thing about the town of Santa Barbara, which now includes some thirty-seven thousand people, is the very wide interest in good architecture extending even to the building of commercial structures and small homes. The people are "architecture" minded and they have become so largely because of the excellent educational work done over a period of years by the Better Homes Committees and the Plans and Planting Branch of the Community Arts Association under the able leadership of Bernhard Hoffmann and Miss Pearl Chase. The Community Arts has been fortunate in receiving for several years a grant from the Carnegie Corporation of New York. Notable results have been obtained by the Association which also includes a fine School of Arts and splendid Music and Drama branches. The effectiveness of such organization and educational work in the arts, and particularly as applied to architecture and gardening, is proved by Santa Barbara's winning the first prize in the national Better Homes in America Campaign for four successive years, 1925 to 1928.

An opportune thing perhaps was the earthquake of 1925 which damaged two-thirds of the old and ugly business buildings of the town, and a few of the old dwellings. It was afterwards proved that only slight damage was sustained by those buildings where the proper amount of cement was used in the mortar to make a good bond.*

A more rigid building code based on the experience of this disaster now protects the city. After the earthquake the city council

Note—Following a suggestion first made in Santa Barbara, Palos Verdes Art Jury has obtained adoption of the following resolution by many civic bodies in various parts of California, including city planning commissions, school boards, chambers of commerce, etc.:

"Whereas, there is much confusion in the public mind as to the proper designation of the style of architecture now so general in this state, and,

"Whereas, this architecture is of a type peculiarly appropriate to California, and has now been developing here for so many years as to be known the world over as typical of this State; now therefore be it

"Resolved, that this type of architecture shall hereafter be designated as "Californian Style," and that we request our officers and staff to adopt this designation as defined below and to discourage the use of the terms "Mission Style," "Spanish Style" as being unfortunate misnomers for an art which has progressed to a degree in which we all may justly take pride, and be it further

"RESOLVED, that the secretary write our local board of education, library trustees, civic bodies and the newspapers, requesting that they take similar action."

The definition referred to is as quoted above.

immediately set up by ordinance** an Architectural Board of Review, which passed on every application for a building permit over $2500.00, to insure that the proposed structure would be reasonably good in design. In the eight months immediately following this Board acted upon some two thousand applications, and by having proper opportunity to discuss with the owners and architects the plans in the preliminary stages it was able to secure their cooperation so that most of the buildings erected conformed to the Californian style.***

Santa Barbara has pointed the way with this, the first municipal regulation of its kind in the country, which effectively set up a barrier to stop the bad architecture so generally foisted upon us in ignorance and carelessness, but none the less to the everlasting ruin of our cities.

Some Buildings that Stand Out

Great art is always rare. But there is inspiration far beyond the ordinary in a number of Santa Barbara buildings illustrated herein, notably in the Ludington and Heberton houses, in the El Paseo group downtown, in the Lobero Theatre. But all the buildings here shown will be found to have the essential quality of beauty, and of charm, which may be said to indicate the soul of a structure. Historically, Casa de la Guerra, with its three sided patio, the Carrillo adobe and the Mission stand out. They are old, lovely, tinged with the spirit of romance, but they cannot claim to be as great examples of architecture as those first mentioned above.

Romance ran riot in the new Court House. It has an extraordinary number of intriguing bits of design, even if the scale is too large, too forced to seem to belong to the happy intimate style of Santa Barbara.

The outdoor reading room of the Public Library is charming (and much used). Sheltered on all sides from the ocean breezes, it is a practical adjunct not often enough provided by libraries in warm climates.

*Note—See "Ten Million Dollars Lost for Lack of a Proper Building Code," in American City Magazine for October, 1925.

**For text of this ordinance see "Progress in Architectural Control" by the present writer, published by the National Conference on City Planning, Washington, 1927.

***A community drafting room privately sustained greatly increased the effectiveness of the Architectural Board of Review.

The most pleasant reaction one gets from public buildings is that produced by the little Museum of Natural History, hidden away among the sycamores and oaks in Mission Canyon. Intimate in scale, it seems to be in complete harmony with nature, and the life that it depicts. This is much in contrast with the horrible caverns of museums so distressing to visitors in our big cities, which with their barnlike proportions and ugly backgrounds well nigh destroy the very treasures they are supposed to display.

Overlooking the city in its slender grace, the new tower of St. Anthony's Seminary is a fortunate addition to Santa Barbara's skyline. On close inspection its detail may seem a bit dry, but the mass and warm brown color are extremely good.

Outwardly massive, with a pleasant portico in front, the Lobero Theatre offers a fine interior with odd shaped auditorium, refreshingly different from most such rooms of our time. On the outside the full heavy mouldings around the stage wing recall the same feeling of strength and massiveness that is found on a smaller scale in the Crematorium in Santa Barbara cemetery, designed by the same architect.

The bold yet warm white color of these and most of the other buildings in the California style make them very much alive, forming a fine foil for the glowing terra cotta roofs, which are nearly always laid random, with a few tile purposely kicked up at irregular intervals.

The strongest first impression of the city to visitors undoubtedly is the general prevalence of light colored plaster walls and tile roofs of the buildings on State Street and neighboring business streets. Then one notices the many arcaded buildings and porticoed stores. There are some 18 arcaded structures on State Street and many more buildings with arched fronts glassed in, which may be converted to arcades when the intended street widening moves the curbs back and pushes the sidewalks under the buildings. The Beard Motor Company building on Carrillo Street, with its generous arches and piers was permitted by the city to project out over the sidewalk because it would not interfere with the effective street space needed for traffic. Yet it contributes greatly to the "city picture," that picturesque quality unfortunately so rarely sought after or even understood by American communities.

The interior of the County National Bank and the patio of the San Marcos Building are distinguished architecture. They express a loftiness of feeling, a boldness of treatment and withal a finish which bespeaks deep knowledge, love and appreciation of the world's greatest art.

The Santa Barbara Biltmore Hotel is so beautiful and pleasing, and also so much in the spirit of the town and its setting that one can hardly realize that its purpose is what the name implies. Here one of southern California's finest architects has designed a hostelry really appropriate to its surroundings and in scale with the residential community. There is restfulness and peace and harmony in every part of it, without loss of dignity. It has many entrancing details to hold one's interest. Here the roof tile have been graduated in color, with the dark tile at the eaves grading up to the very light terra cotta at the ridges. The result is most happy, because of the gradation in tone which is so well done that it blends without being conscious of the transition.

Where gardens are so much used as part of the house, as they are in Southern California the year 'round, the line between architecture and landscaping disappears and the houses tend more and more when properly designed, to become actually a part of the garden. The McAdoo house expressed this, as do many of the others herein illustrated.

Thus a Californian architecture emerges. It is the product of many Architects, inspired alike by the play of sunshine on light surfaces and the contrast of deep shadows, and by the possibilities of heightened effects through the use of varied plant material. Above all it is indigenous to this climate and setting. It has no place in the cold northern regions of snow and ice.

With but few exceptions eastern architects have not understood the precedent set for Californian architecture, nor have they obtained distinction in their designs here. Therefore, the success of the present

Californian style is due almost entirely to the achievement of the architects of California. A notable exception is the late Bertram G. Goodhue. In the design of the J. Waldron Gillespie, 1896, and the Henry Dater houses in Santa Barbara, and later in the buildings of the San Diego Exposition, in 1914, Mr. Goodhue first developed a new and appropriate design based on historic precedent and existing climatic conditions. Since then California's own architects have evolved a new and fitting mode of design, slowly but consistently built upon the best of the past, and that which developed under similar climatic conditions along the Mediterranean and elsewhere.

Mr. Staats is to be congratulated on the reproductions here assembled. They undoubtedly give the larger part of the best examples of Californian architecture in Santa Barbara. It is obviously impossible for him to show everything, nor is it necessary, because here is more than sufficient to illustrate a style now become as distinctive as any single character of structure found in the United States today.

CHARLES H. CHENEY, A.I.A.

Palos Verdes Estates
California.

Introduction to the New Edition by David Gebhard

Three events occurred at the end of the 1920s in the California coastal enclave of Santa Barbara which stand forth as landmarks in this community's effort to develop an "appropriate" architecture for itself. These were the completion of the Santa Barbara County Courthouse, (William Mooser and Co., J. Wilmer Hersey; Ralph T. Stevens, landscape architect, 1925–29); the beginning of the construction of the Fox Arlington Theatre, (Edwards and Plunkett, 1929–31); and the publication of Henry Philip Staats' *Californian Architecture in Santa Barbara*, published by the Architectural Book Publishing Co., Inc. of New York.

The Courthouse and the Fox Arlington Theatre mark a culmination of the efforts of the Plans and Planning Committee of the County Arts Association to revamp Santa Barbara's image into that of a Spanish Mediterranean village.[1] The first of these efforts had its beginning in the construction of extensive villas and gardens in suburban Montecito to the east in the year immediately after 1900. In the Post World War I years, attention had then turned to the city itself, with the development of De La Guerra Plaza as the new small scale civic center for the community. The visual and historic game played around this Plaza entailed utilizing several existing early nineteenth century adobes, including the famed Del La Guerra Adobe, which were incorporated into the new public and private development.

---

1. David Gebhard, *Santa Barbara—The Creation of a New Spain in America* (Santa Barbara: University Art Museum, University of California, 1982); David Gebhard, "Introduction," Rebecca Conard and Christopher H. Nelson, *Santa Barbara: A Guide to El Pueblo Viejo* (Santa Barbara: Capra Press, 1986): 9–23.

The 1925 earthquake turned out to be a godsend which forced the community to rebuild much of its commercial downtown in, of course, the Spanish Colonial Revival/Mediterranean mode. The design and building of a Spanish or Mediterranean villa and its gardens on the hills of the Riviera overlooking Santa Barbara, or within the wooded enclaves of Montecito or Hope Ranch, were essentially a private affair which demanded only taste and wealth to carry it out. To remold an existing city into a new architectural and landscape image was entirely another matter. The architectural transformation of Santa Barbara from a visually chaotic typical small American city to a Spanish Colonial Revival City was, then, as now, an affair unique to the American experience. Newly planned California cities such as Rancho Palos Verdes, Rancho Santa Fe or San Clemente could be projected as communities with a single architectural and landscape theme. But to alter an older existing city—even a smaller one—was, and still remains so today, a formidable political and legal task.

This was, though, the task taken on by Santa Barbara's Plans and Planning Committee under the strong direction of Bernard Hoffmann and Pearl Chase. They perceptively understood that their task was to educate and gently cajole the community into seeing the advantages to be gained by creating a "New Spain in America." From the beginning they were aware that their goals had as much to do with planning, as with individual buildings and gardens. They brought in the planner Charles H. Cheney, an associate of Olmsted and Olmsted, to work closely with them on drawing up new city and county ordinances, to design and plan, and to be a consultant on architectural questions.[2] By 1928, the transformation of the city and the surrounding area was apparent to all. Its revamped image was discussed in the leading national and regional architectural journals, in the popular upper middle class shelter magazines and even by Herbert Hoover, soon to become the President of the United States.[3]

Though whole issues of magazines had been devoted to the His-

2. Pearl Chase, "Bernard Hoffmann—Community Builder," *Noticias* V:2, Summer, 1959: 6–7. Letter of T. Mitchell Hastings, AIA, to Abram Garfield, First Vice President, AIA, in the Pearl Chase Collection, Special Collections, The Library, University of California, Santa Barbara.

3. Charles H. Cheney, "Architectural Control," *The American Architect* 140, (April 1931): 23.

panic transformation of Santa Barbara, Pearl Chase and Bernard Hoffmann felt that there was a pressing need to solidify and sum it all up in a single publication.[4] Such a volume would continue to provide those living in the community with examples to be emulated, and it would solidify the desirability of continuing the tradition on into the decades ahead. In writing to Bernard Hoffmann on May 29th, 1929, Pearl Chase saw the book as advancing ". . . your program for the development of an appropriate architecture in Santa Barbara."[5]

For this projected volume, Pearl Chase prevailed on Henry Philip Staats, a new and young member of the Plans and Planning Committee, to serve as its editor. Staats had come to Santa Barbara and Montecito in the late twenties, and eventually he designed and supervised the construction of several residences, his most widely known being the Montecito villa for F. Day Tuttle of New York, completed in 1934.[6] Staats was trained in architecture at Yale University, graduating in 1924. After leaving Santa Barbara he established his own practice in Litchfield, Conn. in 1932. His assignment in regard to the book was to select and assemble the illustrative material, including photographs and drawings. He was assisted in this by Pearl Chase and Charles H. Cheney. Chase wrote to Cheney on February 4th, 1929, that Staats ". . . had included most of the material that you had suggested."[7] In commenting on the book to Hoffmann somewhat later in 1929, she wrote, "It is also interesting to think that probably no one in Santa Barbara has seen all that is pictured in the volume, not even Mr. Staats."[8]

The organization of the book certainly bears the strong imprint of the way in which Hoffmann and Chase had presented and argued

4. Irving K. Morrow, "A Step in California Architecture," *The Architect and Engineer* 70 (August 1922): 46–103; Irving K. Morrow, "The New Santa Barbara," *The Architect and Engineer* 86 (July 1926): 42–8.

5. Pearl Chase, letter to Bernard Hoffmann, dated May 29, 1929, in the Pearl Chase Collection, Special Collections, The Library, University of California, Santa Barbara.

6. Letters between Pearl Chase and Henry Philip Staats are to be found in the Pearl Chase Collection, Special Collections, The Library, University of California, Santa Barbara. For Staats' view of architectural practice in California see his article: "Clients and Climate," *California Arts and Architecture* 39 (February 1931): 54 and 68.

7. Letter of Pearl Chase to Charles H. Cheney, dated February 4, 1929, in the Pearl Chase Collection, Special Collections, The Library, University of California, Santa Barbara.

8. Letter of Pearl Chase to Bernard Hoffmann, dated May 29, 1929, in the Pearl Chase Collection, Special Collections, The Library, University of California Santa Barbara.

their case for a unified Santa Barbara architecture and landscape architecture throughout the twenties. The supposed legitimacy of the Hispanic tradition for Santa Barbara, (though the source for this architecture was in fact derived more from southern Spain, than from Mexico and Hispanic California), was attested to by initially presenting the principal historic Spanish and Mexican buildings of the community—the great Mission Church and its remaining dependencies, and then several of the principal adobes. The presentation jumps to the 1920s with the depiction of public buildings, institutional buildings, commercial buildings and finally to residences. Though the residential section occupies well over half of the volume, the intent and effort was to portray a total community—from gasoline service stations to public buildings and to great villas and their gardens.

While a good number of major designs of the twenties in Santa Barbara utilized images other than the Hispanic/Mediterranean, none of these was included in this volume. In the sense of what Santa Barbara was about, these non-Hispanic/Mediterranean designs were mistakes, albeit at times tolerated, even handsome mistakes. Charles H. Cheney made this abundantly clear in his preface where he set down, as a series of guidelines, what was meant by the cultivated twentieth century Hispanic/Mediterranean image which was seen as specific to Santa Barbara. Cheney and others had at the time coined the style "Californian Architecture" to describe this new twentieth century verison of the Spanish/Mediterranean tradition.

Thus, *California Architecture in Santa Barbara* turned out to be a summation of a decade of effort to redesign an entire community within the confines of a single image; and it also had ended up, as its author and sponsors had hoped, as the principal source book for the future development of the city and its environs.

CONTENTS

RESIDENCES

Photographs for this book were made by the following Santa Barbara Photographers:

CARL OBERT

J. WALTER COLLINGE

P. H. GREENE

JESSIE TARBOX BEALS

THE GLEDHILLS

FAULDINGS

SANTA BARBARA MISSION
Founded 1786

RESTORED BY ROSS MONTGOMERY,
ARCHITECT.

COVARRUBIAS ADOBE

EL CUARTEL

CASA DE LA GUERRA

CARRILLO ADOBE

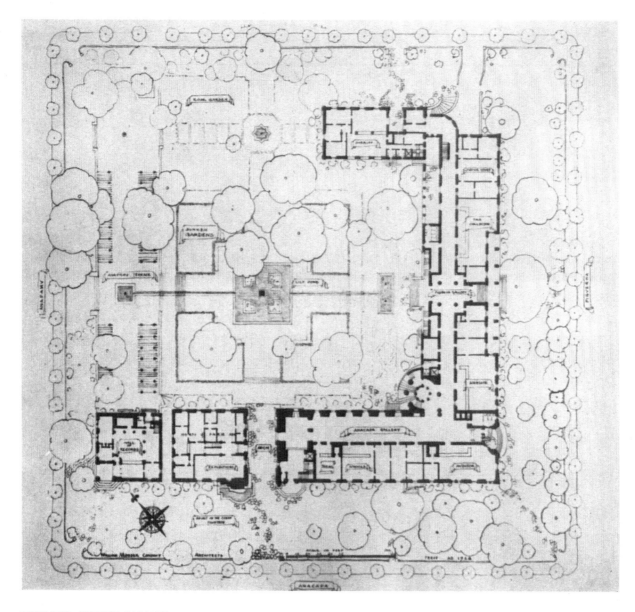

COUNTY COURT HOUSE

WILLIAM MOOSER CO.,
ARCHITECTS.

MUNICIPAL BUILDINGS

WILLIAM MOOSER CO.,
ARCHITECTS.

5

COUNTY COURT HOUSE
Models

MUNICIPAL BUILDINGS

Sketch of Facade

COUNTY COURT HOUSE
Sketch of detail

WILLIAM MOOSER CO.,
ARCHITECTS.

MUNICIPAL BUILDINGS

COUNTY COURT HOUSE

WILLIAM MOOSER CO.,
ARCHITECTS.

7

PUBLIC LIBRARY

WILSON & HORNBOSTEL,
CARLETON WINSLOW,
ARCHITECTS.

MUNICIPAL BUILDINGS

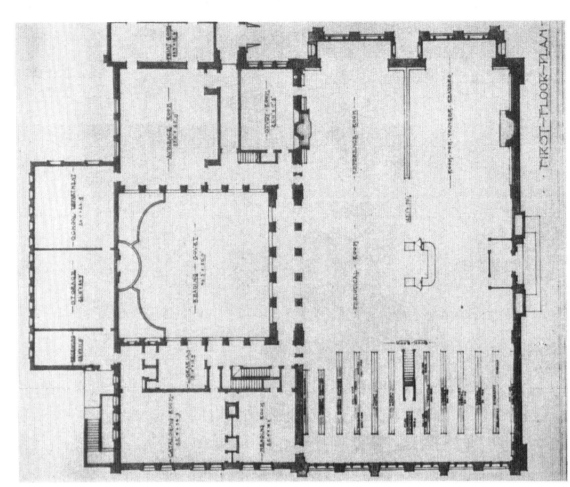

FIRST FLOOR PLAN

WILSON & HORNBOSTEL,
CARLETON WINSLOW,
ARCHITECTS.

9

PUBLIC LIBRARY
Entrance Detail

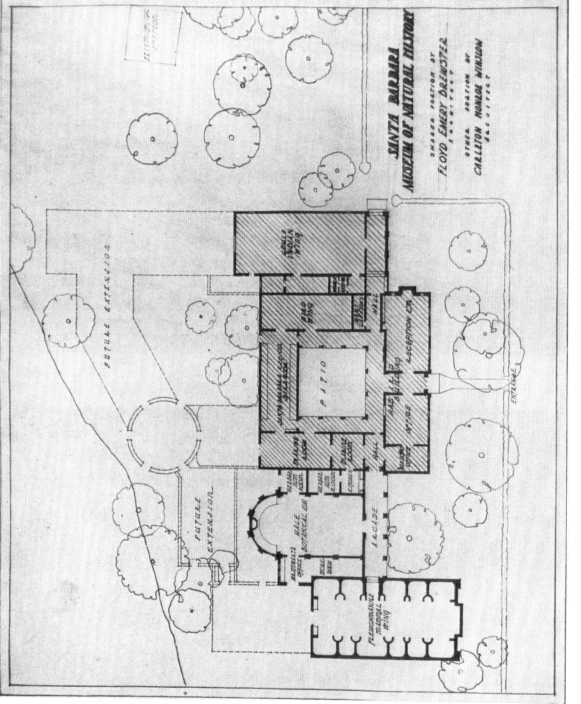

SANTA BARBARA MUSEUM OF NATURAL HISTORY

FLOYD EMERY BREWSTER,
CARLETON MONROE WINSLOW,
ARCHITECTS.

FLOYD EMERY BREWSTER,
CARLETON MONROE WINSLOW,
ARCHITECTS.

MUSEUM OF NATURAL HISTORY

11

MUSEUM OF NATURAL HISTORY

FLOYD EMERY BREWSTER,
CARLETON MONROE WINSLOW,
ARCHITECTS.

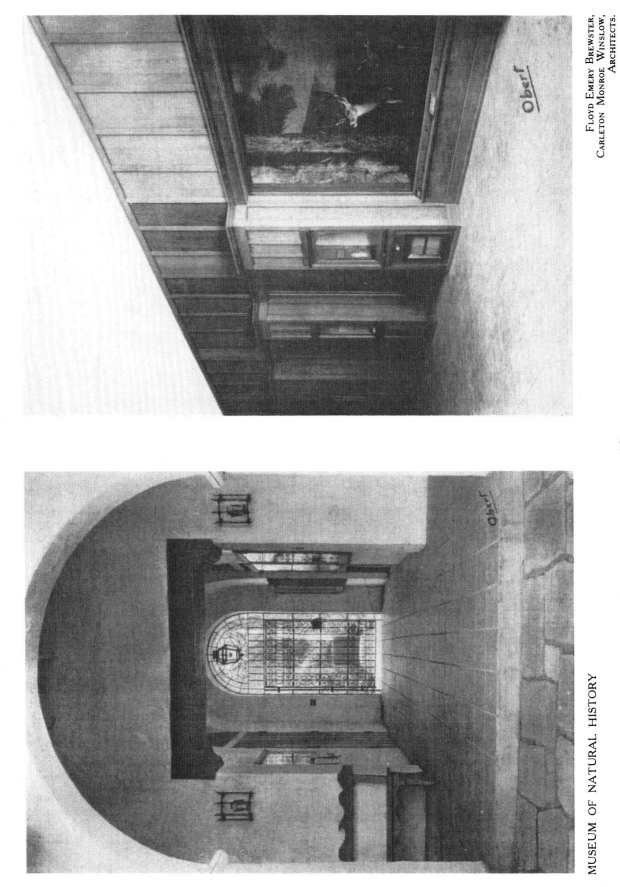

MUSEUM OF NATURAL HISTORY

FLOYD EMERY BREWSTER,
CARLETON MONROE WINSLOW,
ARCHITECTS.

13

MUNICIPAL BUILDINGS

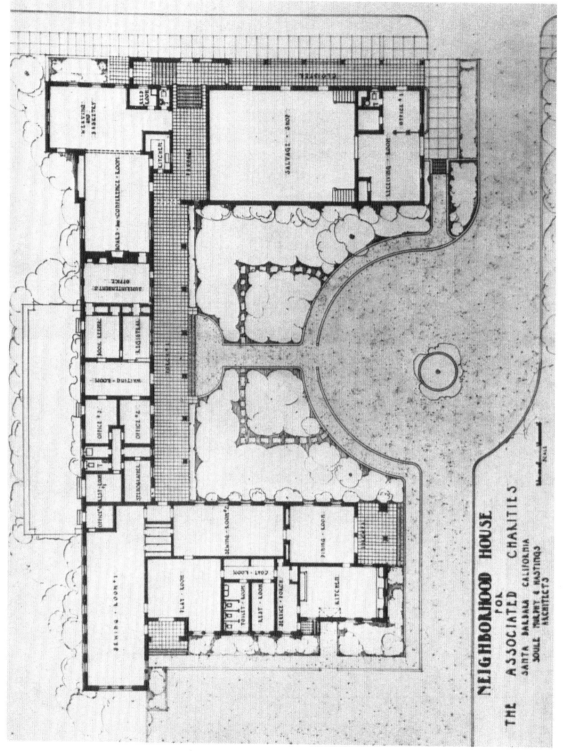

NEIGHBORHOOD HOUSE
for
THE ASSOCIATED CHARITIES
SANTA BARBARA CALIFORNIA
SOULE MURPHY & HASTINGS
ARCHITECTS

SOULE, MURPHY & HASTINGS,
ARCHITECTS.

14

NEIGHBORHOOD HOUSE

NEIGHBORHOOD HOUSE

SOULE, MURPHY & HASTINGS,
ARCHITECTS.

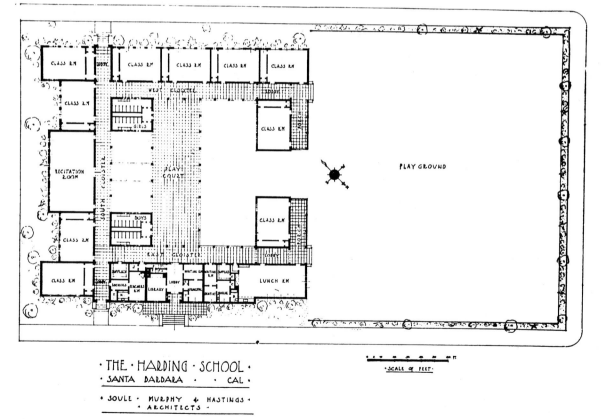

·THE·HARDING·SCHOOL·
·SANTA·BARBARA· ·CAL·
·SOULE· MURPHY & HASTINGS·
·ARCHITECTS·

HARDING PUBLIC SCHOOL

SOULE, MURPHY & HASTINGS,
ARCHITECTS.

HARDING PUBLIC SCHOOL

SOULE, MURPHY & HASTINGS,
ARCHITECTS.

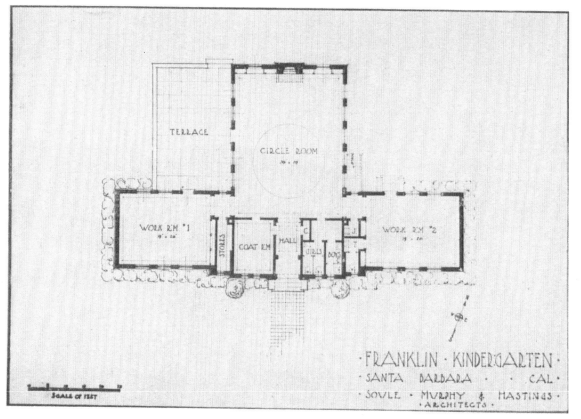

FRANKLIN KINDERGARTEN

SOULE, MURPHY & HASTINGS,
ARCHITECTS.

ST. ANTHONY'S SEMINARY

Ross Montgomery,
Architect.

19

Ross Montgomery,
ARCHITECT.

ST. ANTHONY'S SEMINARY

ST. ANTHONY'S SEMINARY
Altar

ROSS MONTGOMERY,
ARCHITECT.

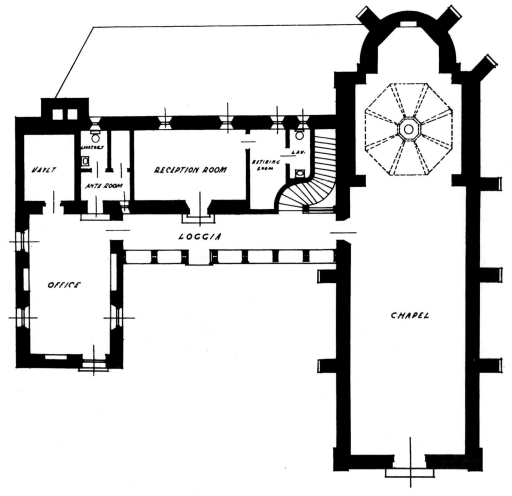

VAULT

LAVATORY

ANTE ROOM

RECEPTION ROOM

RETIRING ROOM

LAV.

OFFICE

LOGGIA

CHAPEL

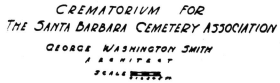

CREMATORIUM FOR
THE SANTA BARBARA CEMETERY ASSOCIATION
GEORGE WASHINGTON SMITH
ARCHITECT
SCALE

CREMATORIUM

GEO. WASHINGTON SMITH,
ARCHITECT.

23

CHURCHES, CLUBS, THEATERS

GEO. WASHINGTON SMITH,
ARCHITECT.

CREMATORIUM

24

MONTECITO COUNTRY CLUB

BERTRAM GOODHUE, ARCHITECT.
(Alterations by) GEO. W. SMITH.

CHURCHES, CLUBS, THEATERS

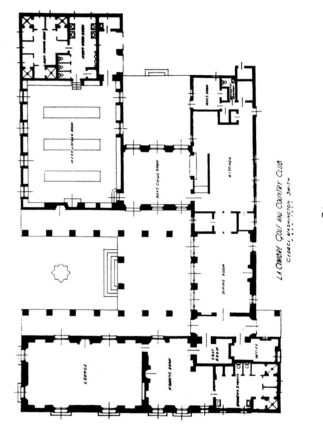

LA CUMBRE GOLF AND COUNTRY CLUB
GEORGE WASHINGTON SMITH

GEO. WASHINGTON SMITH,
ARCHITECT.

26

LA CUMBRE COUNTRY CLUB

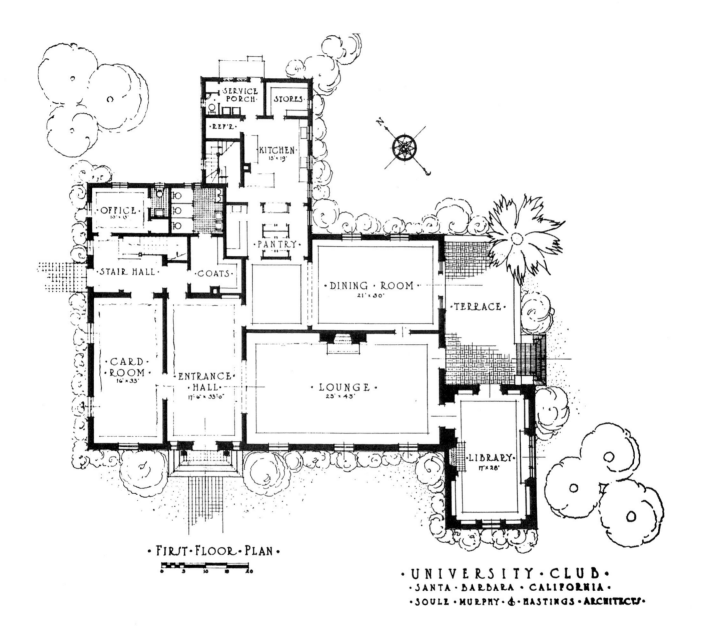

· FIRST · FLOOR · PLAN ·

· UNIVERSITY · CLUB ·
· SANTA · BARBARA · CALIFORNIA ·
· SOULE · MURPHY · & · HASTINGS · ARCHITECTS ·

UNIVERSITY CLUB

SOULE, MURPHY & HASTINGS,
ARCHITECTS.

LITTLE TOWN CLUB

GEO. WASHINGTON SMITH,
ARCHITECT.

29

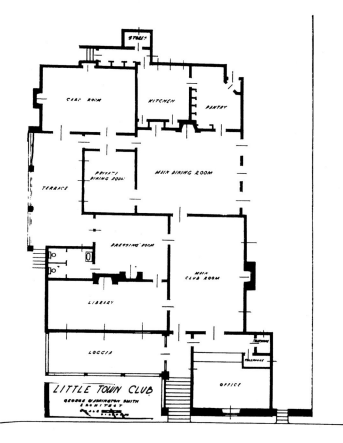

LITTLE TOWN CLUB

Geo. Washington Smith,
Architect.

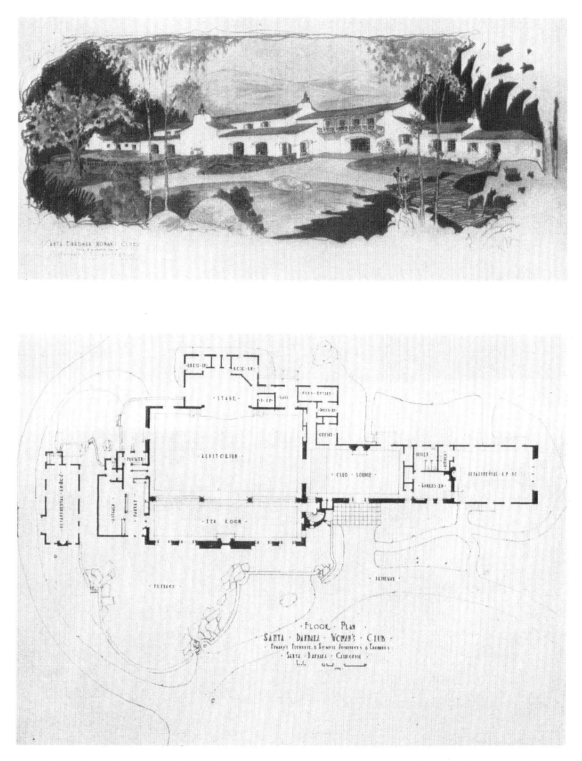

SANTA BARBARA WOMAN'S CLUB

EDWARDS, PLUNKETT & HOWELL,
ARCHITECTS.

SANTA BARBARA WOMAN'S CLUB

EDWARDS, PLUNKETT & HOWELL,
ARCHITECTS.

LOBERO THEATER

GEO. WASHINGTON SMITH,
ARCHITECT.

LOBERO THEATER

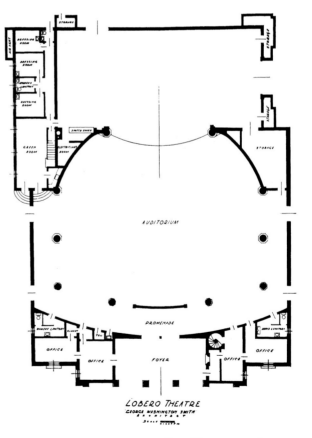

GEO. WASHINGTON SMITH,
ARCHITECT.

CASA DE LA GUERRA

DE LA GUERRA STUDIOS

JAMES OSBORNE CRAIG,
ARCHITECT.

ROOFS   *Photograph by Jessie Tarbor Beals*

PASEO DE LA GUERRA

Photograph by Green
JAMES OSBORNE CRAIG,
ARCHITECT.

DE LA GUERRA STUDIOS

James Osborne Craig,
Architect.

DE LA GUERRA STUDIOS

Photograph by Jessie Tarbor Beals
JAMES OSBORNE CRAIG, ARCHITECT.

38

COMMERCIAL BUILDINGS

ROGERS BUILDING

SOULE, MURPHY & HASTINGS,
ARCHITECTS.

THE COPPER COFFEE POT

EDWARDS, PLUNKETT & HOWELL,
ARCHITECTS.

SALSBURY FIELD BUILDING

EDWARDS, PLUNKETT & HOWELL,
ARCHITECTS.

MERIDIAN STUDIOS

GEORGE WASHINGTON SMITH,
ARCHITECTS.

CLINIC OF MEDICAL ARTS

EDWARDS, PLUNKETT & HOWELL,
ARCHITECTS.

EL CASTILLO

WYTHE, BLAINE & OLSON,
ARCHITECTS.

COMMERCIAL BUILDINGS

Myron Hunt,
Architect.

COURT OF SAN MARCOS BUILDING

42

COUNTY NATIONAL BANK

MYRON HUNT,
ARCHITECT.

SOUTHERN PACIFIC ROUNDHOUSE

ASSOCIATED ARCHITECTS.

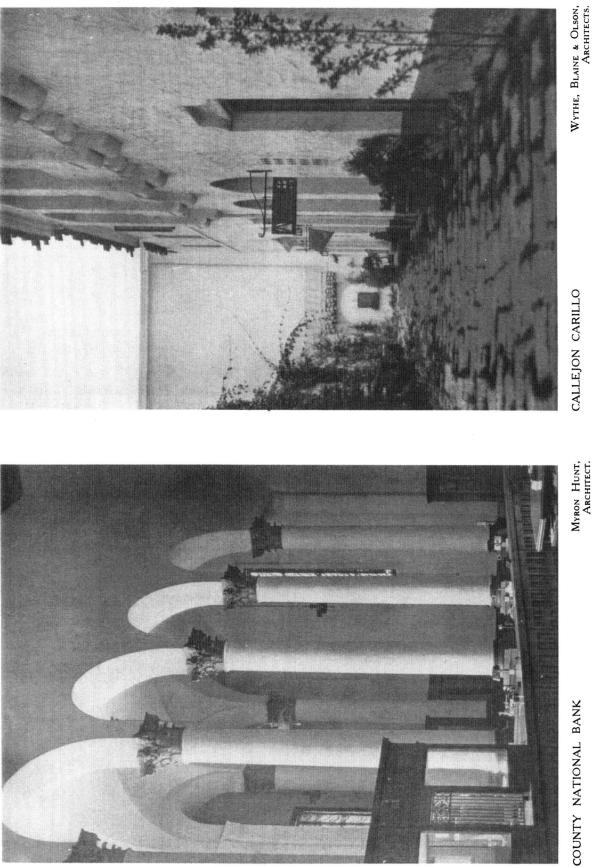

COMMERCIAL BUILDINGS

CALLEJON CARILLO

WYTHE, BLAINE & OLSON,
ARCHITECTS.

COUNTY NATIONAL BANK

MYRON HUNT,
ARCHITECT.

44

COMMERCIAL BUILDINGS

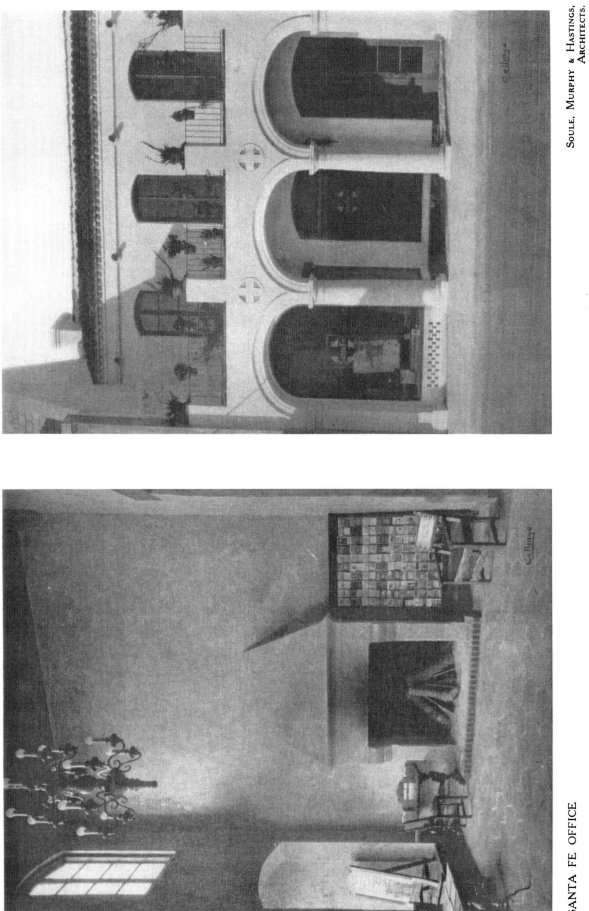

Soule, Murphy & Hastings,
Architects.

SANTA FE OFFICE

45

THE DAILY NEWS

GEO. WASHINGTON SMITH,
ARCHITECT.

CHAMBER OF COMMERCE

ASSOCIATED ARCHITECTS.

BEARDS AUTOMOBILE CO.

Mrs. J. Osborne Craig,
Architect.

JOHNSTON CAFETERIA

Edwards, Plunkett & Howell,
Architects.

STANDARD OIL FILLING STATION

EDWARDS, PLUNKETT & HOWELL,
ARCHITECTS.

48

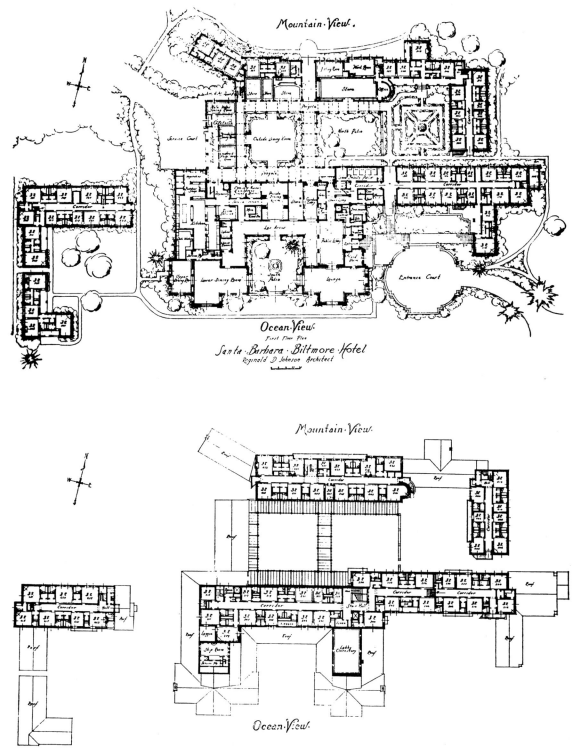

Mountain·View·

Ocean·View·
First Floor Plan
Santa·Barbara·Biltmore·Hotel
Reginald D Johnson Architect

Mountain·View·

Ocean·View·

Second Floor Plan

BILTMORE HOTEL

REGINALD JOHNSON,
ARCHITECT.

BILTMORE HOTEL

Reginald Johnson,
Architect.

BILTMORE HOTEL

REGINALD JOHNSON,
ARCHITECT.

BILTMORE HOTEL

REGINALD JOHNSON,
ARCHITECT.

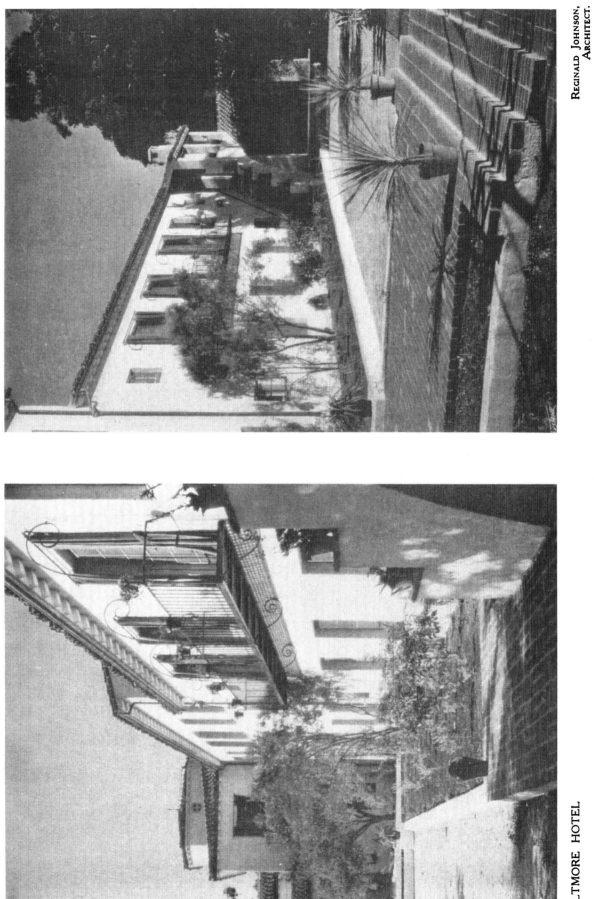

BILTMORE HOTEL

REGINALD JOHNSON,
ARCHITECT.

53

RESIDENCE OF WRIGHT S. LUDINGTON

BERTRAM GOODHUE,
ARCHITECT.

RESIDENCE OF WRIGHT S. LUDINGTON

BERTRAM GOODHUE,
ARCHITECT.

RESIDENCE OF WRIGHT S. LUDINGTON

BERTRAM GOODHUE,
ARCHITECT.

LOCKWOOD DEFOREST, JR.,
LANDSCAPE ARCHITECT.

RESIDENCE OF WRIGHT S. LUDINGTON

57

RESIDENCES

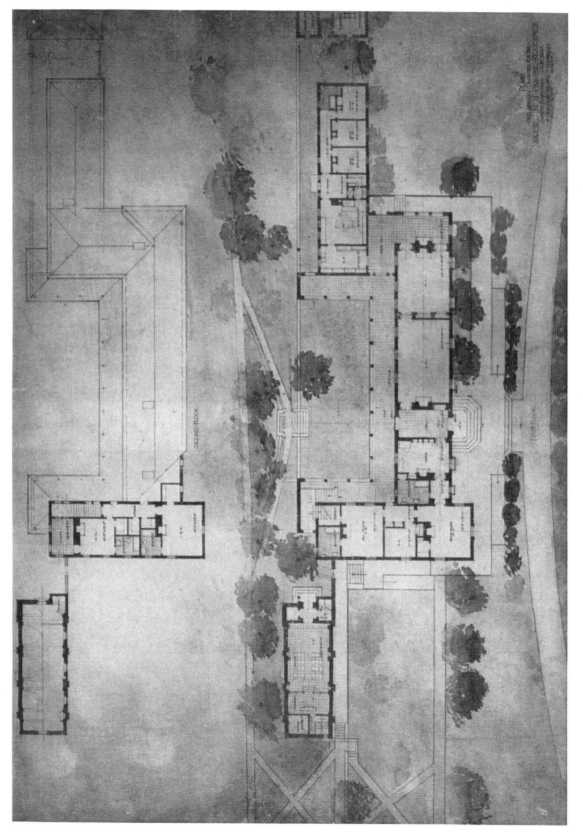

RESIDENCE OF MRS. JOHN H. H. PESHINE

MYRON HUNT,
ARCHITECT.

58

RESIDENCE OF MRS. JOHN H. H. PESHINE

MYRON HUNT,
ARCHITECT.

RESIDENCE OF MRS. JOHN H. H. PESHINE

MYRON HUNT,
ARCHITECT.

RESIDENCE OF MRS. JOHN H. H. PESHINE

MYRON HUNT,
ARCHITECT.

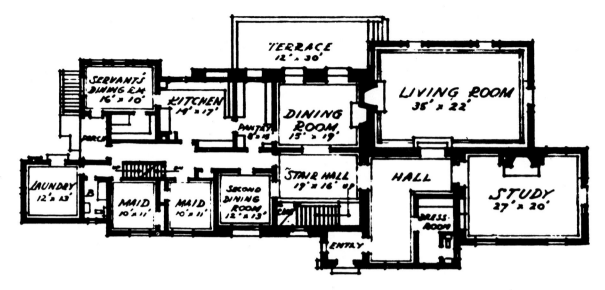

FIRST FLOOR PLAN

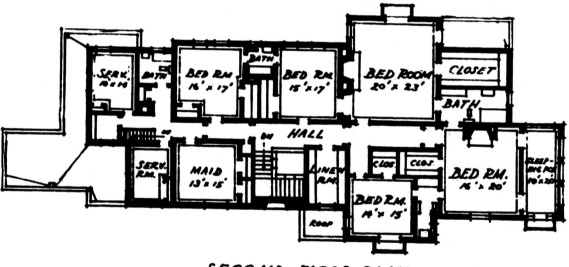

SECOND FLOOR PLAN

RESIDENCES

RESIDENCE OF MR. & MRS. E. PALMER GAVIT

REGINALD JOHNSON,
ARCHITECT.

63

RESIDENCE OF MR. & MRS. E. PALMER GAVIT

REGINALD JOHNSON,
ARCHITECT.

RESIDENCE OF MR. & MRS. E. PALMER GAVIT   Addition by Geo. Washington Smith,
                                                                ARCHITECT.

RESIDENCE OF MR. & MRS. E. PALMER GAVIT   Reginald Johnson,
                                                                ARCHITECT.

RESIDENCES

RESIDENCE OF MR. & MRS. E. PALMER GAVIT

Reginald Johnson, Architect.
Additions By
Geo. Washington Smith, Architect.

66

RESIDENCE OF MR. & MRS. E. PALMER GAVIT   Addition by Geo. Washington Smith,
ARCHITECT.

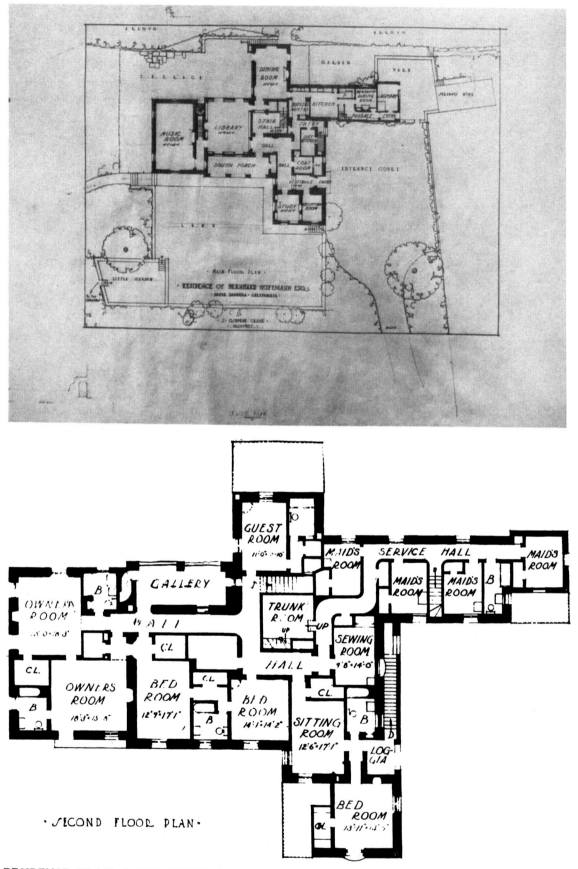

RESIDENCE OF MR. & MRS. BERNHARD HOFFMANN

JAMES OSBORNE CRAIG,
ARCHITECT.

RESIDENCE OF MR. & MRS. BERNHARD HOFFMANN

JAMES OSBORNE CRAIG,
ARCHITECT.

RESIDENCE OF MR. & MRS. BERNHARD HOFFMANN

JAMES OSBORNE CRAIG,
ARCHITECT.

RESIDENCE OF MR. & MRS. BERNHARD HOFFMANN

JAMES OSBORNE CRAIG,
ARCHITECT.

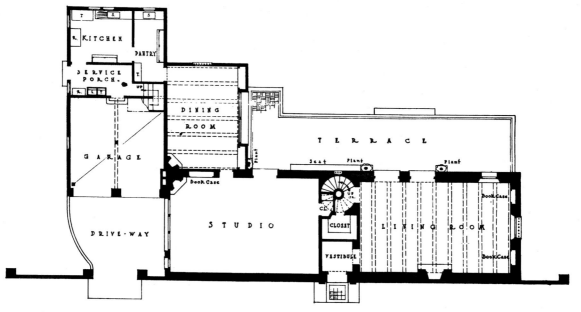

FIRST FLOOR PLAN

RESIDENCE OF MRS. CRAIG HEBERTON

GEO. WASHINGTON SMITH,
ARCHITECT.

RESIDENCE OF MRS. CRAIG HEBERTON

GEO. WASHINGTON SMITH,
ARCHITECT.

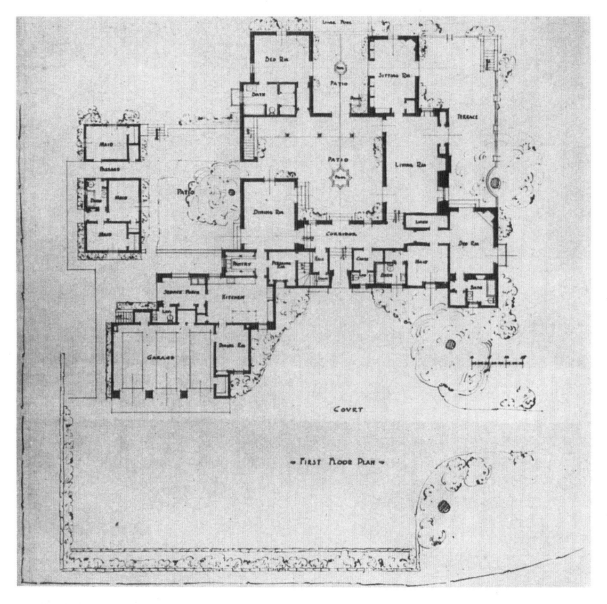

RESIDENCE OF WILLIAM SLATER

MRS. JAMES OSBORNE CRAIG,
ARCHITECT.

RESIDENCE OF WILLIAM SLATER

MRS. JAMES OSBORNE CRAIG,
ARCHITECT.

RESIDENCE OF WILLIAM SLATER

MRS. JAMES OSBORNE CRAIG,
ARCHITECT.

RESIDENCES

RESIDENCE OF WILLIAM SLATER

MRS. JAMES OSBORNE CRAIG,
ARCHITECT.

77

RESIDENCE OF MR. & MRS. JOHN PERCIVAL JEFFERSON

REGINALD JOHNSON,
ARCHITECT.

RESIDENCE OF MR. & MRS. JOHN PERCIVAL JEFFERSON

REGINALD JOHNSON,
ARCHITECT.

RESIDENCE OF MR. & MRS. JOHN PERCIVAL JEFFERSON

REGINALD JOHNSON,
ARCHITECT.

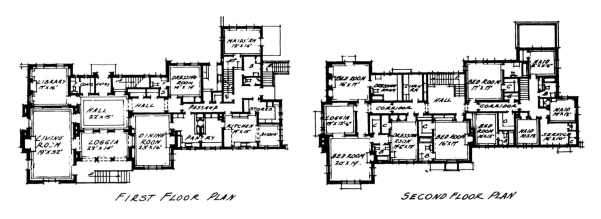

FIRST FLOOR PLAN   SECOND FLOOR PLAN

SCALE

RESIDENCE OF MR. & MRS. EDWARD LOWE   REGINALD JOHNSON,
                                             ARCHITECT.

RESIDENCES

RESIDENCE OF MR. & MRS. EDWARD LOWE

Reginald Johnson,
Architect.

82

RESIDENCE OF MR. & MRS. EDWARD LOWE

REGINALD JOHNSON,
ARCHITECT.

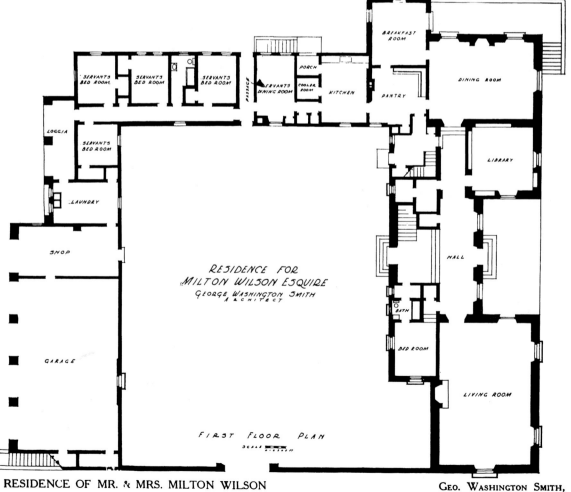

RESIDENCE FOR
MILTON WILSON ESQUIRE
GEORGE WASHINGTON SMITH
ARCHITECT

FIRST FLOOR PLAN
SCALE

RESIDENCE OF MR. & MRS. MILTON WILSON

GEO. WASHINGTON SMITH,
ARCHITECT.

84

RESIDENCES

RESIDENCE OF MR. & MRS. MILTON WILSON

GEO. WASHINGTON SMITH,
ARCHITECT.

85

RESIDENCE OF MR. & MRS. MILTON WILSON

GEO. WASHINGTON SMITH,
ARCHITECT.

RESIDENCE OF MR. & MRS. MILTON WILSON

Geo. Washington Smith,
Architect.

RESIDENCE OF MR. & MRS. MILTON WILSON

GEO. WASHINGTON SMITH,
ARCHITECT.

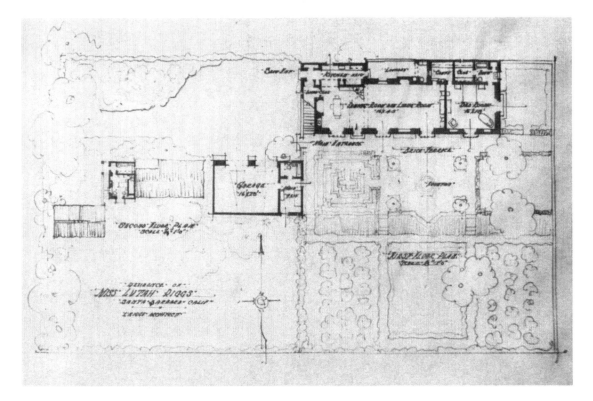

RESIDENCE OF MISS LUTAH RIGGS

Lutah Riggs, Architect—of the office of
Geo. Washington Smith.

RESIDENCES

RESIDENCE OF MISS LUTAH RIGGS

LUTAH RIGGS,
ARCHITECT.

90

RESIDENCE OF MRS. EDWARD CUNNINGHAM

GEO. WASHINGTON SMITH,
ARCHITECT.

RESIDENCE OF MRS. EDWARD CUNNINGHAM

GEO. WASHINGTON SMITH,
ARCHITECT.

RESIDENCE OF MRS. EDWARD CUNNINGHAM

GEO. WASHINGTON SMITH,
ARCHITECT.

93

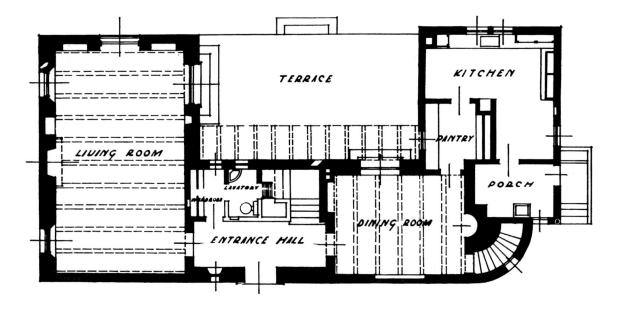

FIRST FLOOR PLAN
RESIDENCE FOR
MISS MARGARET BURKE
GEORGE WASHINGTON SMITH
ARCHITECT

SCALE

RESIDENCE OF THE MISSES BURKE

GEO. WASHINGTON SMITH,
ARCHITECT.

RESIDENCE OF THE MISSES BURKE

Geo. Washington Smith,
Architect.

RESIDENCES

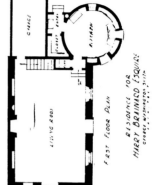

SECOND FLOOR PLAN

FIRST FLOOR PLAN

RESIDENCE FOR
HARRY BRAINARD ESQUIRE
GEORGE WASHINGTON SMITH

RESIDENCE OF MR. HARRY BRAINARD

GEO. WASHINGTON SMITH,
ARCHITECT.

96

RESIDENCE OF MR. HARRY BRAINARD

GEO. WASHINGTON SMITH,
ARCHITECT.

97

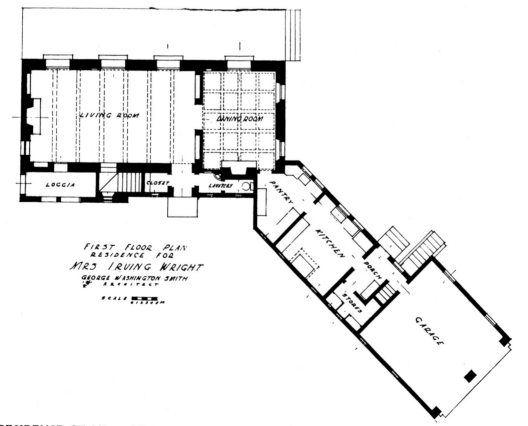

FIRST FLOOR PLAN
RESIDENCE FOR
MRS IRVING WRIGHT
GEORGE WASHINGTON SMITH
ARCHITECT

SCALE

RESIDENCE OF MR. & MRS. IRVING WRIGHT

GEO. WASHINGTON SMITH,
ARCHITECT.

RESIDENCE OF MR. & MRS. IRVING WRIGHT

GEO. WASHINGTON SMITH,
ARCHITECT.

99

RESIDENCES

RESIDENCE OF MR. & MRS. IRVING WRIGHT

Geo. Washington Smith,
Architect.

100

RESIDENCE OF MR. & MRS. WILLIAM GIBBS McADOO

CARLETON WINSLOW,
ARCHITECT.

RESIDENCES

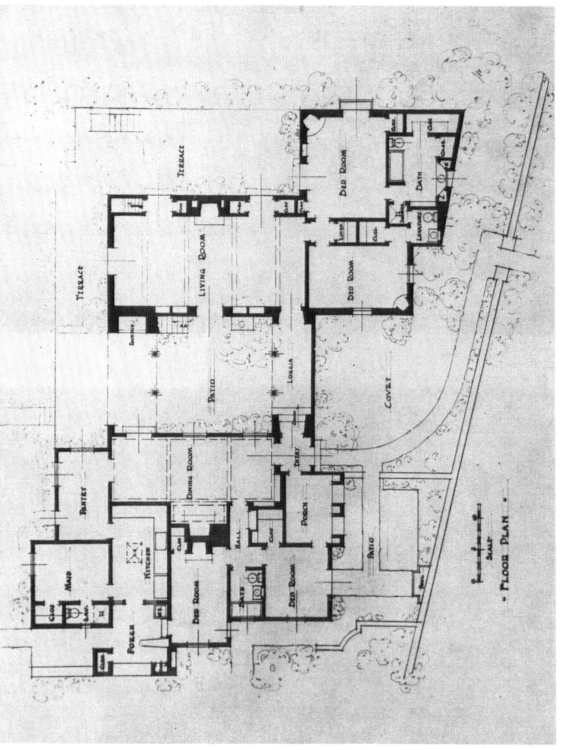

RESIDENCE OF MRS. JAMES OSBORNE CRAIG

MRS. JAMES OSBORNE CRAIG,
ARCHITECT.

102

RESIDENCE OF MRS. JAMES OSBORNE CRAIG

MRS. JAMES OSBORNE CRAIG,
ARCHITECT.

RESIDENCE OF MRS. JAMES OSBORNE CRAIG

Mrs. James Osborne Craig,
Architect.

RESIDENCES

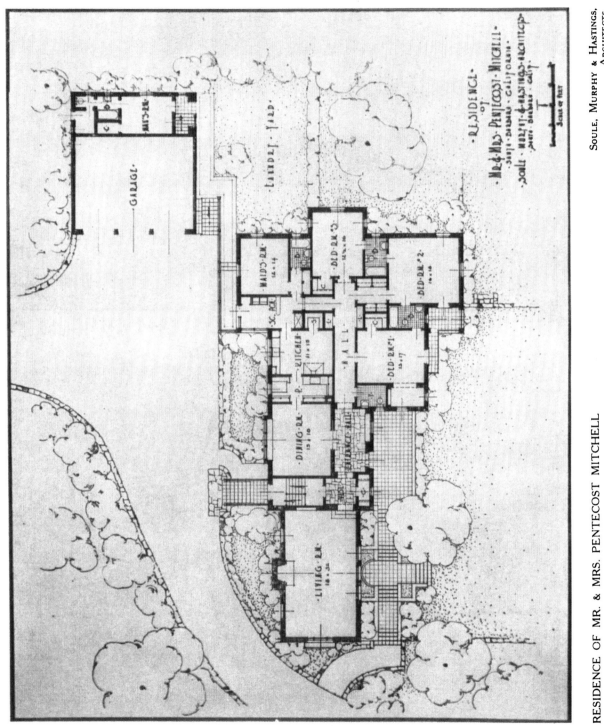

RESIDENCE OF MR. & MRS. PENTECOST MITCHELL

SOULE, MURPHY & HASTINGS, ARCHITECTS.

105

RESIDENCE OF MR. & MRS. PENTECOST MITCHELL

SOULE, MURPHY & HASTINGS, ARCHITECTS.

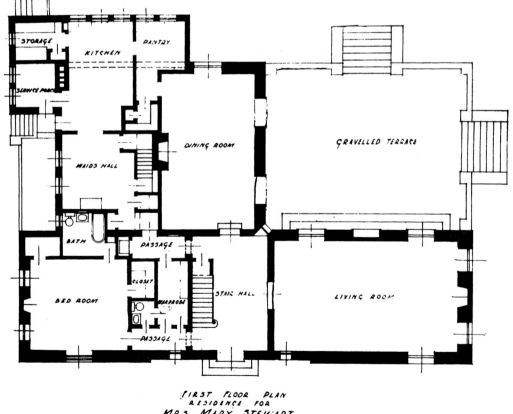

FIRST FLOOR PLAN
RESIDENCE FOR
MRS MARY STEWART
GEORGE WASHINGTON SMITH
ARCHITECT

RESIDENCE OF MRS. MARY STEWART

GEO. WASHINGTON SMITH,
ARCHITECT.

RESIDENCES

RESIDENCE OF MRS. MARY STEWART

Geo. Washington Smith,
Architect.

108

RESIDENCE OF MRS. MARY STEWART

GEO. WASHINGTON SMITH,
ARCHITECT.

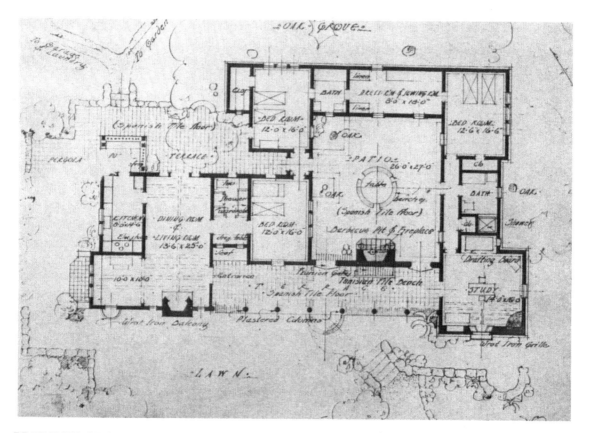

RESIDENCE OF MR. & MRS. FLOYD BREWSTER

FLOYD BREWSTER,
ARCHITECT.

RESIDENCE OF MR. & MRS. FLOYD BREWSTER

FLOYD BREWSTER,
ARCHITECT.

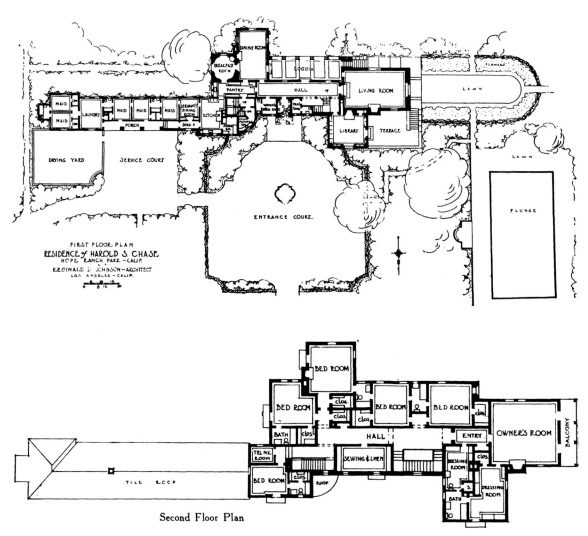

FIRST FLOOR PLAN
RESIDENCE of HAROLD S. CHASE
HOPE RANCH PARK - CALIF.
REGINALD D. JOHNSON - ARCHITECT
LOS ANGELES - CALIF.

Second Floor Plan

RESIDENCE OF MR. & MRS. HAROLD STUART CHASE

REGINALD JOHNSON,
ARCHITECT.

RESIDENCE OF MR. & MRS. HAROLD STUART CHASE

REGINALD JOHNSON,
ARCHITECT.

RESIDENCE OF MR. & MRS. HAROLD STUART CHASE

REGINALD JOHNSON,
ARCHITECT.

114

RESIDENCE OF MR. & MRS. HAROLD STUART CHASE

REGINALD JOHNSON,
ARCHITECT.

BARN ON ESTATE OF E. J. MILEY

Mrs. James Osborne Craig,
Architect.

RESIDENCE OF MR. & MRS. GEORGE McCONNEL

Leonard Cooke,
Architect.

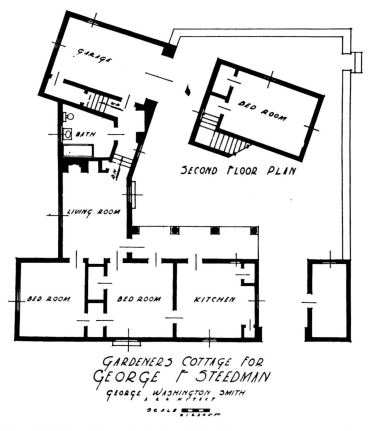

GARDENER'S COTTAGE, ESTATE OF GEO. F. STEEDMAN

Geo. Washington Smith,
Architect.

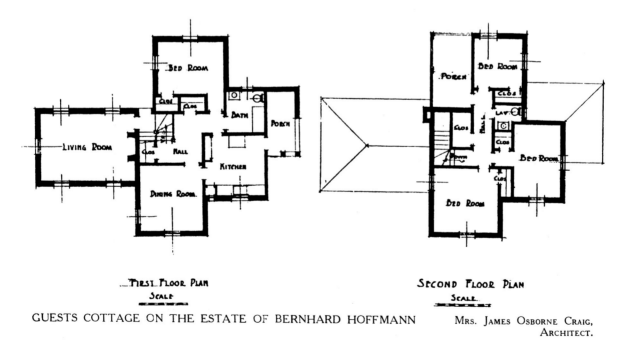

FIRST FLOOR PLAN
SCALE

SECOND FLOOR PLAN
SCALE

GUESTS COTTAGE ON THE ESTATE OF BERNHARD HOFFMANN

MRS. JAMES OSBORNE CRAIG,
ARCHITECT.

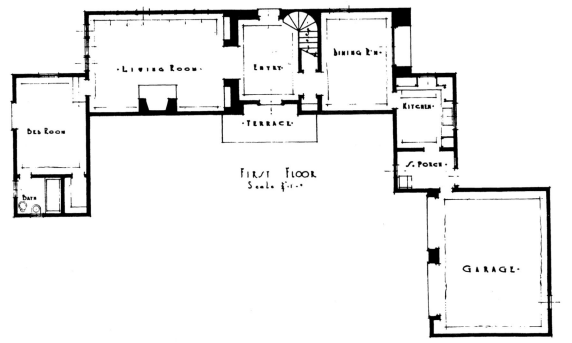

FIRST FLOOR
Scale ⅛"=1'-0"

RESIDENCE OF MR. & MRS. JAMES MacKAY

EDWARDS, PLUNKETT & HOWELL,
ARCHITECTS.

RESIDENCE OF MRS. J. C. ANDREWS

EDWARDS, PLUNKETT & HOWELL,
ARCHITECTS.

FIRST·FLOOR·PLAN

·RESIDENCE·FOR·DR·MARIAN·WILLIAMS·
·SANTA·BARBARA· · ·CALIFORNIA·

·SECOND·FLOOR·PLAN·

·SOULE·MURPHY·&·HASTINGS·
·ARCHITECTS·

RESIDENCE FOR DR. MARIAN WILLIAMS

SOULE, MURPHY & HASTINGS,
ARCHITECTS.

121

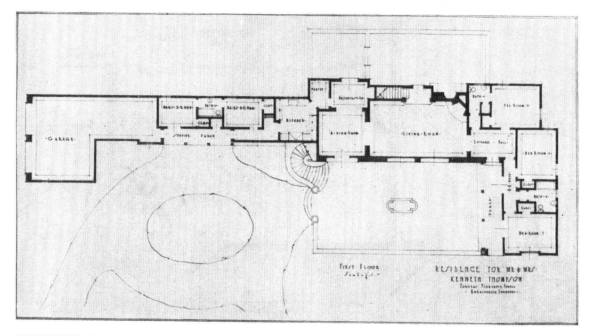

RESIDENCE OF MR. & MRS. KENNETH THOMPSON

EDWARDS, PLUNKETT & HOWELL,
ARCHITECTS.

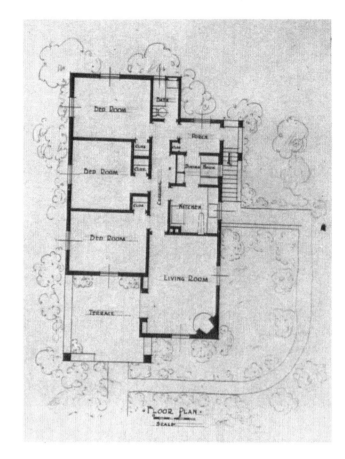

CHAUFFEUR'S COTTAGE ON ESTATE OF JOHN P. JEFFERSON   Mrs. James Osborne Craig,
ARCHITECT.

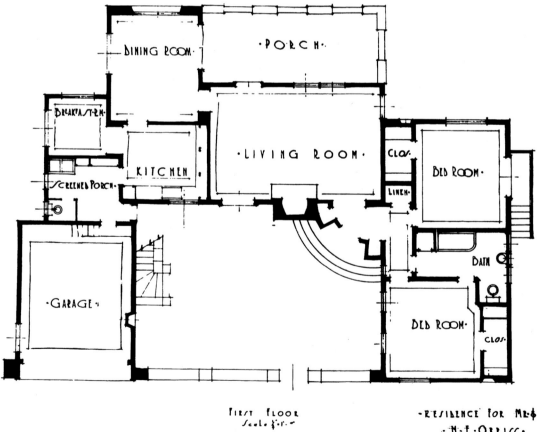

·FIRST FLOOR·
Scale ⅛"=1'-"

·RESIDENCE FOR MR & MRS·
·H·E·ORISS·
·EDWARDS· PLUNKETT & HOWELL·
·ARCHITECTS & ENGINEERS·

RESIDENCE OF MR. & MRS. H. E. ORISS

EDWARDS, PLUNKETT & HOWELL,
ARCHITECTS.

RESIDENCE OF MR. & MRS. WILLIAM C. PAULTON

BERTRAND HARMER,
ARCHITECT.